Blue Star, New Star

Matthew C. Fleenor, PhD

Archway Publishing books may be ordered through booksellers or by contacting:

Archway Publishing
1663 Liberty Drive
Bloomington, IN 47403
www.archwaypublishing.com
1 (888) 242-5904

Because of the dynamic nature of the Internet, any web addresses or links contained in this book may have changed since publication and may no longer be valid. The views expressed in this work are solely those of the author and do not necessarily reflect the views of the publisher, and the publisher hereby disclaims any responsibility for them.

Any people depicted in stock imagery provided by Getty Images are models, and such images are being used for illustrative purposes only.
Certain stock imagery © Getty Images.

ISBN: 978-1-4808-8913-2 (sc)
ISBN: 978-1-4808-8915-6 (e)

Print information available on the last page.

Archway Publishing rev. date: 09/26/2020

ARCHWAY
PUBLISHING

sun star   one star
here star   near star

how we wonder what they are
is best known from our one star
plasma is the word to know
spots and fields the sun will show

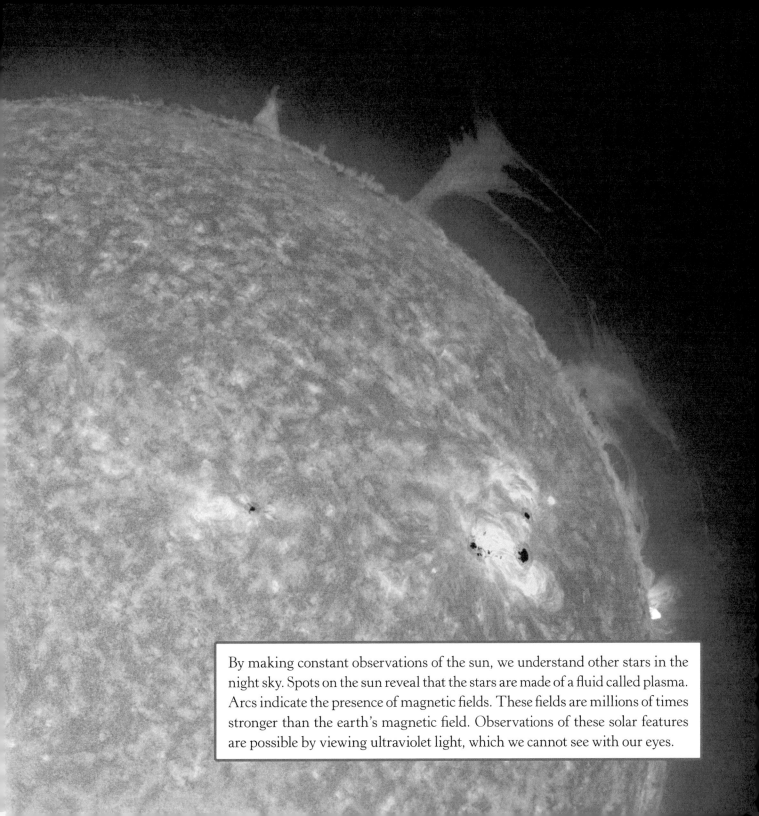

By making constant observations of the sun, we understand other stars in the night sky. Spots on the sun reveal that the stars are made of a fluid called plasma. Arcs indicate the presence of magnetic fields. These fields are millions of times stronger than the earth's magnetic field. Observations of these solar features are possible by viewing ultraviolet light, which we cannot see with our eyes.

black star   orange star
green star   brown star

color shows the star's degree
its surface is a black-body
color tells us cool or hot
blue is hot and brown is not

is it a star
or a planet?

Brown dwarfs are called "failed stars" because they do not begin fusion. Astronomers determine the star's color by connection with a surface temperature (called a blackbody curve). The color "brown" defines a blackbody that is cool. In almost all of the images in this book, the appearance of the objects has been enhanced through "false-color" imaging.

red star   dwarf star
red star   giant star

color is not our only guide
to what is on a star's inside
dwarfs and giants are not the same
knowing stars is not that tame

EARTH

RED DWARF   OUR SUN

RED GIANT

Most stars are found in clustered regions, so the sun is rather unique among stars. Globular clusters (GCs) have tens of thousands of individual stars (see above). Open clusters are much younger than GCs and do not have as many stars (see later page on clusters). GCs provide one way to determine the age of our universe.

x star black star
u star bright star

hidden light from stars can harm
with earth's blanket there's no alarm
telescopes up in the sky
make plain the hidden to our eye

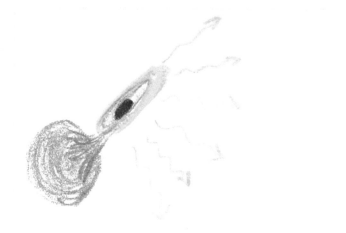

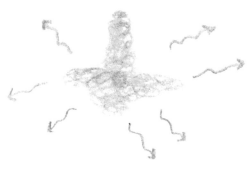

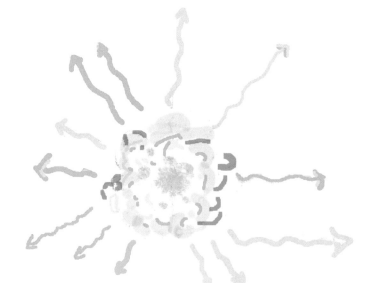

satellite
telescope

Most of the light from stars cannot be seen from earth, and we use satellite telescopes above earth's atmosphere. Harmful X-rays inform us about black holes (or black stars). Even though the black star does not emit light, the disk that surrounds the black star releases the X-rays we detect (as shown above).

spot star   spin star
bulge star   wind star

stars spin slow and stars spin fast
mass determines how long they last
most massive stars must give off wind
stuff of stars can't be held in

star wind

star spot

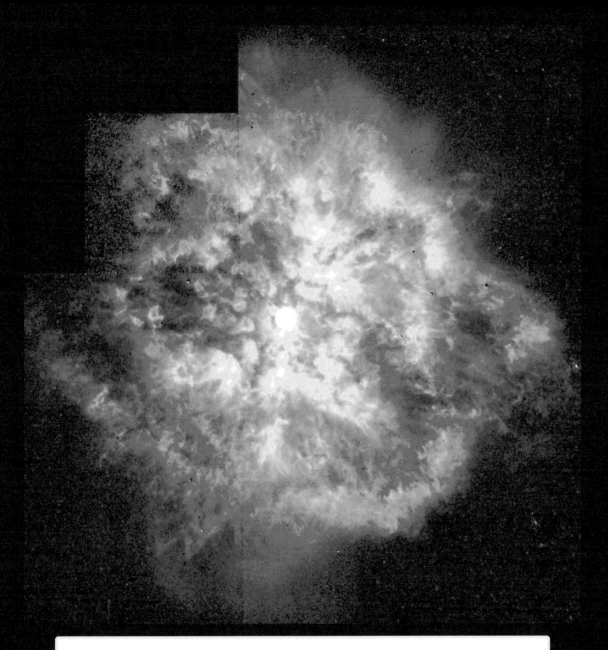

Activity in stars is observed through rotation of star spots and winds. Some stars are so bright that pieces of the star are carried away from the surface. This is called a stellar wind. Our sun star has a small wind but not as powerful as the star here. These stars are short lived because they are so big.

one star   two star
three star   four star

clumps of gas and clusters too
have stars in number not a few
the sun star is a special case
since most are in a crowded place

GLOBULAR
CLUSTER

OPEN
CLUSTER

Open clusters contain hundreds of new, blue stars that reveal a young age. The surrounding red gas is false-color imaging of the cloud remnants from which these stars formed (see next page). The long points coming from each star are diffraction spikes caused by the telescope mounting and not the stars.

cloud star   gas star
dust star   mass star

stars are born like you and I
in a cloud beyond the sky
their lives are long compared to us
ten million years without a fuss

NEBULA = star cloud

1000 LY
100 million AU
100,000,000 AU

sun

earth

1 AU = 93 million miles

|←— 1 AU —→|

Stars are born in clouds of gas called a stellar nursery. The nearest stellar nurseries are in our Milky Way galaxy, though still far away from our sun-star. A light year is the distance light travels in one year, which is equal to 100 million times the earth-sun distance (AU)!

blue star   new star
red star   old star

stars are born and stars get old
many secrets stars do hold
ageing stars puff out in red
it's like a person's graying head

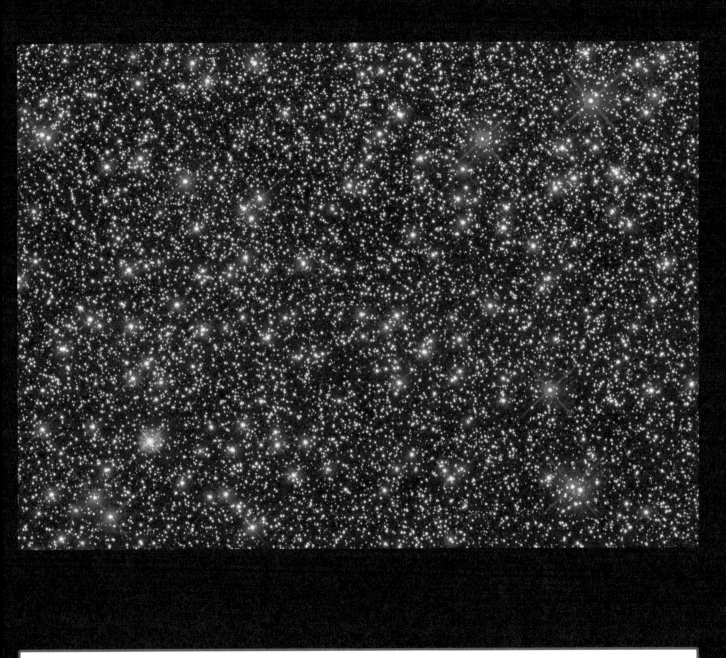

Stars have different sizes and colors. Most blue stars are younger, while most red stars are older, though there are exceptions to this rule. A star "puffs out" when it becomes a red giant. When our sun-star becomes a red giant, its size will extend past our earth orbit.

blue star full star
red star change star

gas inside makes stars bright
fusion gives stars their light
atoms simple, atoms small
changing atoms give stars all

HYDROGEN ATOMS

PHOTON, PACKET OF ENERGY

hf

hf

HELIUM ATOM

Stellar evolution is the term given to the process of how stars change over time. Most of the changes result from new elements forming within the core of stars. Fusion is the process of forming more massive elements from less massive ones. Through fusion, hydrogen is converted into helium.

rock star   show star
draw star   you star

atoms make up you and me
stars form atoms we can see
elements within star's core
supernova make stars roar

Fusion continues in massive stars until iron is produced. Iron is a stable element and cannot fuse. Since fusion supports the star against gravitational forces, this support is removed. The stellar core collapses, which is one way to produce a supernova. Because these processes provide elements for life as we know it, it is often that we are "star stuff."

three star   bear star
five star   lion star

stars connected by our eye
make up patterns in the sky
though not real, patterns fun
animals — can you find one?

Patterns with stars we create are called asterisms, while official patterns are constellations. They are like state and country boundaries for the night sky. Most stars in the night sky are not actually close to one another, yet constellations are helpful to astronomers and observers alike. One popular association is the Pleiades (above).

where star there star
port star guide star

stars are wondrous there's no doubt
but when you're lost, stars help out
around the world as sailors roam
stars that guide one to their home

Celestial navigation, guiding by star positions, was of great importance many hundred years ago. As time-keeping devices improved, celestial navigation was not needed. The night sky is a reliable tool for directing yourself in primitive conditions, but you have to begin by looking up on a regular basis.

Citations References:

Matthew C. Fleenor, PhD, is an astronomer, educator of undergraduate physics and astronomy at Roanoke College, and father of three. Much of his work at Roanoke provides the opportunity to communicate complex astronomical concepts to undergraduate nonscience majors and the public. He seeks to build wonder in everyone toward the natural world as a teacher, parent, and human. He currently lives in Virginia.

Printed in the United States
By Bookmasters